Your Persona... The Mask You Wear

Understanding Your Personality Traits

What is your Personality Channel and why does it matter?

CONSTANCE SANTEGO

Books Constance has written

The Intuitive Life
A Guide to Self Knowledge & Healing
through Psychic Development

Fairy Tales, Dreams and Reality...
Where are you on your path?

Your Persona... The Mask You Wear
Understanding Your Personality Traits
What is your Personality Channel and why does it matter?

When I teach a workshop I begin with the four channels: Audio, Knower, Feeler and Visual. I describe some of the personality traits and characteristics that are in each, and I explain how each channel learns and loves. Then I demonstrate how to muscle test a person by selecting someone from the audience, and I write out theirs and their family's channels. I'll explain how they all get along, who fights with whom, who is probably divorced (and who probably caused it), who is the loudest /quietest, who is the black sheep, who needs what kind of love, how they learn, and so much more. I muscle test a wide variety of people from the audience to showcase the importance of understanding these four channels.

I have helped many people who were having marriage difficulties (love, finances, and habits, to name a few issues). I have helped many, many students, parents, and teachers understand their learning style (channel), and shown them how to adjust to maximize the knowledge they retain. I have helped many people on a spiritual level; we die with our memories stored in our soul, not our brain. If you believe in the afterlife, understanding the four main channels will help you communicate.

Understanding the channels will help you with your relationships, your income, and your sanity, simply by knowing yourself that much better!

They say "Happy wife, happy life". I say "Happy self, happy life".

Ease of communication is the key!
Are you an Audio, Knower, Visual, or Feeler?

Constance Santego

I would like to dedicate this book to my husband
for his patience and encouragement while I wrote it.
I Love you! Here is a big hug.

To my Mom, who always knew this was the book...

And a very special thanks to all my students and clients over the years.

Table of Contents

Prologue

The blue spot light was on her, the warmth from the light inspired her to take a breath and play her role.

She had beautifully sexy eyes that were made up to look like a goddess. Her hair was dark and reached her shoulders, with bangs over her forehead that accented her eyes. Her head was adorned with a web of jewels that sparkled in the light as she moved. She wore a floor length gown that seemed enchanted, so silky smooth with a sash around her slim waist. Her feet were cradled by the softest leather sandals.

Many called her 'Majesty', some braved 'Queen', but very few ever called her by name... Cleopatra, Queen of the Nile. She was born into an era that required strength and hope.

Love... we all seem to secretly desire riches, fame and success. Some need to see Love, they wear it to show it in so many ways. Some need to feel Love by touch or actions. Others need to hear or speak Love, which is the most literal use of the word. There are some who just know and never seem to have to justify receiving or giving... they Love time itself.

The actress playing Cleopatra knew that all four channels mattered for her to excel at her part in the play. Love... anyone could see it, and just being around her you could feel it. She spoke with words and wisdom from within... a confident inner beauty that shone through in how she spoke, how she moved, what she wore, and how she knew it.

Understanding your personality traits and how to achieve all your wishes, wants, and desires begins with understanding *Your Persona... The Mask You Wear.*

Many people have many different masks, and some wear more than one in a single day. Mother, brother, doctor, dentist, streetwalker... we all wear a mask, some because we were born into that role, some by addictions, necessity or freak accident, and others by ascension and determination. No matter how you came to your order of the channels you play a part in your theatrical movie called Life.

I am here to share with you the secrets of your personality and why you wear the mask you do... be it the mask of Knower, Audio, Feeler, or Visual. You will learn to command and demand your future – live the life of a Queen, soldier, farmer, scholar, or athlete. No matter what your wishes, wants, and desires are I will grant you knowledge that will empower you through the rest of your life, regardless of whether it's a business or personal affair. Enjoy the heavenly gifts granted to each and every one of us, starting with... *Your Persona... The Mask You Wear*

Understand your personality traits like no other has explained before

•The Mask of a Knower can be as brilliant as Einstein or as slow minded as Forest Gump.
•The Mask of a Visual can be as beautiful as a sunset or as ugly as the wake of war.
•The Mask of a Feeler can be as soft as the kiss of a raindrop on a morning petal or as rough as a storm at sea.
•The Mask of an Audio can be as sweet to the ear as the voice of an angel or as eerie as a harpy.

Life's Spirit, God if you like, has granted us the gift of 'ask and you shall receive'. We all have the power to take off our Mask and try on another, if we so choose.

It starts in the womb and either stays or changes, maybe even a few times as you age. The Mask you wear becomes a product of your environment; family and friends have a large influence. We either believe the part we are given and play it out or we use the spiritual gifts God grants to each and every one of us to change and receive our new role. Gifts like wisdom, knowledge, faith, healing, miracles, prophecy, language, or interpretation.

Wisdom = Wise, heavenly inspired
Knowledge = Mental growth
Faith = Believing in yourself
Healing = Emotional, physical, mental, or spiritual
Miracles = As magical as a mother lifting a car off her baby
Prophecy = Your future awaits
Language = To communicate
Interpretation = To see, feel, hear, and know (by using your senses)

The Mask you wear, your Persona today... it is just as you like it – familiar and safe.
But what if you are seeking more?

I am here!

Personal Note

The road of life has many curves, but what is most interesting is how we handle the corners. Even more exciting is choosing which vehicles to drive.

I have worn a lot of masks in my life so far: daughter, sister, cousin, friend, student, employee, seamstress, laborer, salesperson, mail sorter, esthetician, spa practitioner, volunteer, candy striper, interior designer, wife, mother, aunt, boss, teacher, principal, president, massage therapist, minister, cook, janitor, barista, artist, dancer, finishing carpenter's assistant, author...

No matter what performance I have acted out in real life, my true personality eventually shows through. So what do the vehicles I drive and the masks I wear have in common? They are part of my persona... the role I play in my life.

Audio, Knower, Visual, and Feeler are titles I have named the four personality channels a person uses. Each channel has many traits to distinguish the differences between them, which determines how a person acts or plays the way they do in daily life.

My Persona... my personality channels and traits have been with me since birth. It's in my genetic code and was influenced by the environment I grew up in. The Mask I wear (Visual, Feeler, Audio, or Knower) and the role I play in everyday life is made up of a combination of my personality traits. My personality traits and channels will be a part of me until I die.

This divine knowledge of the Four Personality Channels that make up '*Your Persona...The Mask You Wear*' has greatly improved my life. Many have stated that it has immensely changed their lives, and I'm sure that the knowledge of the order of your channels will give you a better understanding of self, allowing you to improve, adapt, and even change your persona if you want to.

Shift happens... Create magic!
Constance

Introduction

Ever wonder why you react or care about money or love the way you do? What about in school... ever wonder why you don't learn like some of the other class mates? Or how your daily life routines are so different from your family, friends, or associates?

Your Persona...

Your Persona... the mask you were born with matters depending what order your four personality channels are – Audio, Knower, Visual, Feeler; or maybe they are Visual, Feeler, Audio, Knower. Whatever the order is it really does make a difference!

Your Persona, the specific order in which your Four Personality Channels are arranged will tell you exactly how and why you react in a certain way, and even how you love and learn.

What I really enjoy about the four channels of the persona is that they are easy to remember and are exactly what they mean:

Audio – words and sounds
Knower – thoughts and time
Visual – sight and pictures
Feeler – touch and emotions

Over the years you have heard about personality types, but this book is a bit different. '*Your Persona... The Mask You Wear*' is explained from a wisdom and knowledge that dates further back then Cleopatra's time.

Even though we have all the fancy gadgets of today, people still repeat the same passions and crimes, as far back as the bible and even further back than caveman days.

Most of us expect everyone to be just like us. We expect everyone to be able to learn and understand the same way, and if they don't then maybe they're stupid or slow. Be honest here... when you were in high school how many times did you think a classmate was an idiot for asking a question; why were they wasting everyone's time? My guess is they weren't stupid at all, they were just using a different personality channels than you, and maybe even different channels than the teacher was. Over the years, and even if you are now all grown up and mature, I bet that you still sometimes think that someone is an idiot, stupid, or slow... be honest.

'Your Persona... The Mask You Wear' will explain to you in easy, usable terms the four personality channels which people use to express their persona (their personality traits). You will have six different tests, quizzes, and exercises to determine yours, your friend's, families, and even co–worker's main personality channel. Your channels are explained so simply that you can even notice and tell a person's main personality channel just by watching his or her body language, or listening to what words he/she uses when speaking.

Knowing their main personality channel will help you determine how to better communicate with your loved ones, business associates, students, clients, or customers. The bottom line is you will learn better, love better, and make much more money!

Historic Uses of Personality Types, Personality Traits, and Personality Tests

Dictionary Meanings

• A **personality type** approach says whether you are an introvert or an extravert.
• A **personality trait** approach says you can be anywhere on a continuum ranging from introversion to extraversion, with most people clustering in the middle and fewer people towards the extremes.
• A **personality test** is a quiz you take to figure out which personality type you are.

Here we will explain some of the different versions of personality types and traits that you may already know about (in order of the year it was identified in).

Ayurvedic Body Types (over 5000 years old)

From India there are three main Ayurvedic body types (doshas) – Vata, Pita, & Kapha.

Vata	Pita	Kapha
Creativity	Ambition	Caring
Enthusiasm	Concentration	Centeredness
Freedom	Confidence	Compassion
Generosity	Courage	Contentment
Joy	Enthusiasm	Faith
Vitality	Happiness	Fulfillment
	Intelligence	Patience
		Stability
		Support
		Tenderness

The Four Humors

Hippocrates (Age of Pericles - Classical Greece) believed each characteristic was due to an excess of one of four bodily fluids – yellow bile, blood, black bile, and phlegm.

Yellow bile

Organ: spleen
Element: fire
Temperature: hot and dry
Traits: violent, vengeful, short tempered, ambitious
Too much fire makes one choleric

Blood

Organ: liver
Element: air
Temperature: hot and moist
Traits: red-cheeked, corpulent, amorous, happy, generous, optimistic, irresponsible
Too much air makes one sanguine

Black bile

Organ: gall bladder
Element: earth
Temperature: cold and dry
Traits: introspective, sentimental, gluttonous
Too much earth makes one melancholic

Phlegm

Organ: lungs
Element: water
Temperature: cold and moist
Traits: induces passivity, lethargy, subjectivity, devotion and emotionalism
Too much water makes one phlegmatic

As a first step the prudent Hippocratic physician would prescribe a regimen of diet, activity, and exercise, all designed to 'void the body of the imbalanced humor'.

Jungian Types of the Four Temperaments

Carl Jung in 1921 based the types on the strengths and limitations of one's psychological type. (A Swiss psychiatrist, Carl Gustav Jung (26 July 1875 – 6 June 1961) was an influential thinker and the founder of Analytical Psychology).

Extroversion (E)	Introversion (I)
Intuition (N)	Sensing (S)
Thinking (T)	Feeling (F)
Judgment (J)	Perception (P)

Using the letters above, it is possible to have a unique 4 letter code to indicate each. Example: ENFP

Somatotypes

In 1940, William Sheldon classified personality according to body type.

Endomorphy – focused on the digestive system, particularly the stomach (endoderm); has the tendency toward plumpness, corresponds to Viscerotonia temperament traits; tolerant, love of comfort and luxury, extrovert.

Mesophorphy – focused on musculature and the circulatory system (mesoderm), has the tendency towards muscularity, corresponds to the Somatotonia temperament traits; courageous, energetic, active, dynamic, assertive, aggressive, risk taker.

Ectomorphy – focused on the nervous system and the brain (ectoderm) – the tendency towards slightness, corresponds to Cerebrotonia temperament traits; artistic, sensitive, apprehensive, introvert.

Type A / B Personalities

Created by Meyer Friedman, an American cardiologist in 1950

Type A personalities: Are workaholics, always busy, driven, somewhat impatient.
Type B personalities: Laid back and easy going, passive.

Myers–Briggs Type Indicator

Isabel Briggs Myers and her mother, Katharine Briggs, in 1962 developed from Carl Jung's Four Temperaments the Myers–Briggs Type Indicator [instrument], the aim of which was to make the insights of type theory accessible to individuals and groups.

The 16 personality types of the Myers-Briggs Type Indicator® instrument are listed here as they are often shown in what is called a 'type table'.
ISTJ, ISFJ, INFJ, INTJ, ISTP, ISFP, INFP, INTP, ESTP, ESFP, ENFP, ENTP, ESTJ, ESFJ, ENFJ, ENTJ

My Instructors Diploma Program

Converger	Diverger	Accomodator	Assimilator
Challenges Field Trips	Essays Internet	Story Boards Symbols	Catagorizing Research

Here are a few more

- Right Brain, Left Brain
- Four Colors: yellow, blue, red, and green (It started with Max Lûscher, in 1940s).
- Scientology has an IQ Personality test to take before you join (Oxford Capacity Analysis)
- Astrology – fire, earth, air, and water

• One of the most famous personality types are the twelve Sun / Zodiac signs in Western Astrology and Eastern (Vedic) Astrology

Aries
E – April 15 – May 14
W – March 21 – April 19

Taurus
E – May 15 – June 14
W – April 20 – May 20

Gemini
E – June 15 – July 14
W – May 21 – June 20

Cancer
E – July 15 – August 14
W – June 21 – July 22

Leo
E – August 15 – September 14
W – July 23 – August 22

Virgo
E – September 15 – October 14
W – August 23 – September 22

Libra
E – October 15 – November 14
W – September 23 – October 22

Scorpio
E – November 15 – December 14
W – October 23 – November 21

Sagittarius
E – December 15 – January 14
W – November 22 – December 21

Capricorn
E – January 15 – February 14
W – December 22 – January 19

Aquarius
E – February 15 – March 14
W – January 20 – February 18

Pisces
E – March 15 – April 14
W – February 19 – March 20

The common link between all the different personality types in the historic information is that they all explain personality traits.

What is great about the *Your Persona... The Mask You Wear* Series?

• The personality channels are easy to remember: Audio, Knower, Visual, & Feeler
• There are six different types of tests to take
• The personality channels are easy to remember: Audio, Knower, Visual, & Feeler

They can help you:

• Know what job would best suit you or what you need to learn to achieve a better one
• Know what personality channel would make your best soul mate in a relationship
• Know how to learn any subject better
• Understand your partner, children, friends and co–workers much better
• Understand yourself, especially in Love and Learning
• Understand how you save or spend money
• Understand how you express yourself when you are sick
• Understand what makes you happy
• Understand the mask you wear... Your Persona

YOUR PERSONA... WHAT IS IT MADE OF?

THE FOUR PERSONALITY CHANNELS OF COMMUNICATION

Scientists say that we are not born with our personality traits, but that we learn them. I believe each of us is born with our basic personality channels of communication, especially when we are expressing love and/or when we are trying to learn something new.

When a child is born into this world, they will learn how to speak, write, comprehend, and read in one or more traditional languages: Chinese, Spanish, English, Arabic, Hindi, Portuguese, Bengali, Russian, Japanese, German, etc. But a child communicates long before they learn to speak. A child uses many senses to communicate what is needed; crying, grasping, eye movement, and many even believe they can use a type of telepathy.

MOST PEOPLE ARE BORN WITH ALL OF THESE SENSES

Vision (sight)
Auditory (sound)
Kinesthetic (touch and emotion)
Olfactory (smell)
Gustatory (taste)
And some believe Extra Sensory Perception (ESP)

And we communicate through these five (six) senses.

All outside information is processed internally by one or more of these senses. The information is processed in the brain and a response is given back to the external world through our behavior and language.

Even a newborn baby has a persona, his or her own combination of personality traits. A baby expresses his or her personality long before he or she can talk, or even understand why he or she is acting the way he or she is. Ask any maternity nurse if the new born babies have a personality of their own. Ask any parent if their toddler has a personality. Genetics and environment, starting with the information received in the womb, all contribute to a person's persona.

There are many combinations of personality channels, with a varying intensity or degree of each. These make up each person's personality, but the basis of the four channels – Audio, Knower, Visual, and Feeler – will always tell you how one Loves and Learns.

Having a basic understanding of these 'Four Personality Channels of Communication' and in which order you were born with will give you greater insight into your everyday life. You will understand why you do the things you do in the way that you do them, and why your friends, family, coworkers, and acquaintances do things their own way. Reading this book and/or taking a seminar or workshop will teach you how to understand and use that knowledge to better your relationships or to better understand your comprehension skills.

The Four Personality Channels of Communication

When I first started teaching about these channels, back in 1999, I called the four channels Celestial Languages. I felt they were a form of communication that came from the heavens. Over the years, though, people would argue that they were not; English, French, Spanish, Mandarin, etc. were languages. So the best we (there was a discussion) could come up with was the word channel, which is now used for the four ways that an individual person expresses his or her own language.

Dictionary meaning for the word *Channel* – a method or system for communication or expression along or through a specific route or medium.

The Four Personality Channels of Communication titles that I use are

Audio, Knower, Visual, and Feeler

There are many different theories of determining what personality type a person may be, as in the examples given to you previously in the historic section of this book. I believe the Four Personality Channels of Communication are a little different. I've found that people have four specific ways of how they communicate, especially while learning or expressing Love.

Are you familiar with the following terms?

	French for	*My interpretation*
Clairaudience	Clear hearing	Audio
Claircognizance	Clear knowing	Knower
Clairvoyance	Clear seeing	Visual
Clairsentience	Clear feeling	Feeler

Most people can use all four channels, but usually only two are prominent. Please note, one is not better than the other. They are all equal to each other. The point is not to try to be like someone else, but to learn which channel you use the most; which channel your significant other, family, friends, coworkers, or students use so you know how to communicate better.

Your personal combination of the Four Personality Channels make up Your Persona and determine how you perform in everyday experiences.

In Love, Learning, Communicating, and Making Money

Your Persona has a combination of the four Personality Channels of Communication and each channel has very different personality traits which are explained in more detail in...

Traits of the Four Personality Channels of Communication

Audio Channel

Oral and written language
Clairaudience (clear hearing)

Traits of an Audio

- Words are very important
- Love to listen to music
- Hear and understand the lyrics to a song
- Enjoy typing or writing with a pen
- Are very literal, blunt
- Need detailed and factual information
- Love information in a printed format
- Need to have everything in writing, so there is no miscommunication
- Can seem arrogant
- Can be loud
- Childhood toys: play telephones, any type of computer, bang on pots, any thing that makes noise
- Adult toys: computer, ipods, stereos, cell phone, webcam, karaoke, anything that promotes communication
- A cell phone is their life line to the world, they cannot live without a cell phone (probably have more than one)
- Will not turn off their phone(s) unless made to!!!
- Cannot miss a call (even when sleeping – will answer it at any hour)
- Listen to the radio
- Are extremely good at spelling, grammar, and punctuation
- Love languages, probably speak more than one
- If a Poker player, uses textbook rules
- Can be verbally bullying
- Need to hear or read it to believe it
- Their handwriting is long winded and literal
- Will read the instructions on how something works
- For travel/driving directions – use street names, left or right, miles
- Need everything very clear and precise; it is either correct or wrong
- May have done graffiti as a kid
- Love to talk (in person, on the phone and in letters, Facebook, chat

rooms)

• Love to have money in the bank, RSP's, Stocks, etc. (Numbers are facts!)
• If they have an addiction it is only because someone said it was cool

In the shopping mall

- Will only buy brand name items
- Items must be on sale or a great deal!
- Will stop and talk to everyone they know.
- Would bring a friend for their feedback
- Will buy online (ebay, amazon, etc)
- Purchase for fashion and trends

• Automobile; will be new or a classic (great stereo and a great deal)
• Their house will be focused around their sound system and computer
• If they have a tattoo, most likely it will have words and/or sayings on it

Common words used

• Dinner sure sounds good right now
• I hear ya
• Listen to that
• You and I don't speak the same language

Knower Channel

Knowledge / Thought

Claircognisance (clear knowing) spelled also Claircognizant

Traits of a Knower

• Overanalyze/consider all the alternatives, think about all possible scenarios
• Research everything, even a simple purchase
• Usually take days to decide what to do about a decision, idea, or problem
• Are very cautious
• When they know a subject they can give instant recollection of the information
• Can usually sense things ahead (read a situation/intuitive)
• Seem to be calm and have inner peace, unless pushed to respond
• Are aware of the consequences
• Are quiet and soft spoken (unless second language is Audio – then they are a bit of a know-it-all)
• Become self-sufficient and hate to ask for help
• Notice any spelling, grammar, and punctuation errors
• Are usually loners (do not need others)
• Childhood toys: brain stimulant; rubik's cube, one person games
• Adult toys: Scrabble, Sudoku, crossword puzzles, science, books, library, Google, Bridge
• If a Poker player; would not play in person until they know the game inside and out,
    • Plays the odds/calculation of percentages
• With age can be very self-confident
• Usually let others go first while they watch, listen, and get a feel for it to determine if they should do the same
• Hand writing is very clear and readable
• When they know something, they *know* it
• Always over guessing themselves or think themselves out of most things
• If he/she says "*think*" (they do not know it yet) If he/she says "*know*" (they do know the info)
• Listen to the news or read about current events

• Only have a cell phone for emergencies or to access the internet
If they have an addiction it is only to shut out the noise of other people

In the shopping mall

- Only if they have to, they hate the crowds
- Purchase for need and purpose
- Will go to every store to compare items and then go home and think about it
- Would try on everything a few times and still need time to decide
- Their automobile will be useful

• House: will be either dirty or extremely clean, definitely functional
• They would not usually have a tattoo

Common words used

- I know I am hungry for dinner or you know what I like to eat so you decide
- I knew that
- Don't know
- I am thinking
- I don't understand

Visual Channel

Pictorial / Symbols
Clairvoyance (clear seeing)

Traits of a Visual

• Love TV and movies
• Likes art, drawing, painting and colouring
• Need to see how something works to understand it
• Need to see it to believe it
• Every item in the house has a special place
• Usually tells stories when speaking
• Very materialistic and loves nice things
• Travel or driving directions – draws you a map, tells you colours of the buildings around
• Childhood toys: light bright, dress up, barbies, art, beautiful dolls, fireworks, movies
• Adult games: would rather not play, but likes DVD's, Movies, Pictionary, any noncompetitive game that everyone wins at
• If a Poker player: can see and read subtle body language
    • Love the psychology of the game
    • With a good hand gets excited and makes quick decisions
• Need eye contact. Likes to look you in the eyes when talking to you
• Talk very quickly so they do not lose their train of thought
• Talk on more than one subject at a time
• Do not completely finish their sentences, but will make sense by the end of the conversation
• Hate talking for very long periods of time on the telephone; needs to see the person
• Hand writing is usually neat and can be pretty
• Need to spell check everything on the computer or have someone else edit
• Love sticky notes for reminders
• Only have a cell phone for necessity (usually business)
• Love to buy real things, they can see the dollars that are used
• Trust the money they can see
• Notice themselves in pictures, mirrors, or windows

• If they have an addiction it is to escape into another world/story or to look cool

In the shopping mall

- Window displays and store ambiance is very important
- Notice even the slightest changes from last visit
- Change room floors must be clean to try on clothes
- Usually will not buy anything they cannot see in real life
- Notice the clothes on a Mannequins – Oh that looks cute
- If it looks good they may spend over budget, price is not important

• Their automobile: will be good looking, shiny, clean, with good visibility
• House: will be big or showy, looks clean, everything has a place, all rooms have a theme
• Has fine furniture
• Lots of ornaments
• Tattoos would be beautiful and colorful

Common words used

• Dinner would sure look good right now
• I can see that
• See you later
• We don't see eye to eye

<u>Feeler Channel</u>

Kinesthetic/Touch

Clairsentience (clear feeling)

<u>Traits of a Feeler</u>

- Are always busy… go, go, go… can't sit still
- Are great at getting the job done – and quickly
- Are very spontaneous and will try anything once
- Go by their gut feeling
- Love to play sports and be active
- Are very competitive
- Need to use their hands, Love to touch things
- Tell stories with lots of emotion
- Are a bit moody or emotional
- Are very sensitive to taste and texture
- Talk with their hands (even when driving) and very touchy when they talk
- Can be very sensitive to the energy of others, bad or good
- Need to feel it to believe it
- Love the beat of a song (tap along)
- Only have a cell phone for work, to keep in touch with family and friends, or to play games
- Need real money in their pocket
- Are very creative with their hands; wood carving, pottery, models
- Childhood toys: Lego, stuffed animals, forts, cars, anything fast, action figures
- Adult toys: video games, anything fast, sports/fitness, board games, playing cards
- Their hand writing is fast and usually messy
- If a Poker player: Love to play for fun or on the internet
    - Hate to lose in public
    - Gut feeling, either lucky or the odds are against them
    - May not play many hands if not sure if they can win
- Are forgetful, cannot find things easily
- Take a long time to calm down after having an issue
- May sleep walk or act out in their sleep

- If they have an addiction, it is only because it feels good or to not feel at all

In the shopping mall

- Will only notice what they are going in for
- Do not like waiting while someone else shops
- Quick in and out of all stores unless just to walk around (good exercise)
- Food court is the best place
- Usually will not buy anything they cannot touch first
- Purchase for fit and durability

- Their automobile: fast, big, and can go off road
- Their house: will be spacious, comfortable, temperature controlled, inviting, room for all the toys, not always clean
- Tattoos would have a deep meaning and probably would be about another person

Common words used

- I really feel like it
- That taste has a weird texture
- That feels right
- I don't think we are on the same path

So, what Main Channel do you think you are?
Audio, Knower, Feeler, or Visual?

Six Exercises to Determine Your Persona

Time to have some Fun and Test Your Persona...

What is your order?
And more importantly, why does it matter?

Test #1 – Body Movement Exercise

Your body movements will tell you a lot about what main channel you are.

When talking, if your hand(s) move

To your sides	Audio
Around your shoulders or head	Visual
Around your lower or hip area	Feeler
Straight ahead	Knower

(Leg movements, foot movements, and head tilting can also give you more hints to your main channel)

Example: You are in a conversation with your child, friend, family, etc, and you ask them this question... *"What did you do today?"*

Watch what happens to their body movements. (If only their eyes moved then go to the eye movement exercise following). Many people start to talk with their body. Their hands or feet move, or they start to fidget on one side or the other.

• Did they just stare at you without moving a muscle (or eyes) when they answered your question? Did they ask you what you wanted to know? Did they start to move their left foot while talking to you? Left side movement of a foot is a self talk (our right – meaning they are repeating what you just said in their head). Usually a **Knower trait.**

• Did they start to move their right foot while talking to you? Their right (our left) is a **Feeler trait**, meaning they went back into their emotions.

• Did they talk with a hand moving at the side of their body? Left or right hand movement is an **Audio trait.**

• Did they tilt their head up to one side while talking?

Head movement is a **Visual trait**.

There is nothing wrong if they are doing a combination of the movements. It just means this will not be an easy test to decide which personality channel they are.

Test #2 – Muscle Testing (Kinesiology) Exercise

An easier name for this exercise is Body Pendulum, and it's one of my favorites. You will learn to use your body to find out the order of your, a friend's, or your family's personality channels. The brain is like a computer and stores all the information about each individual. When using Muscle Testing, you are programming the brain to answer 'yes' or 'no' to your questions.

Before asking the correct question to determine the personality channel order, here is the Muscle Testing exercise for you to learn:

To start: You will have to physically move your body... Please stand up.
• Have your body lean forward from the ankles (like you are as stiff as a piece of wood) while saying *"Forward without falling is a yes"*, and then lean your body backwards saying *"Backward without falling is a no"*.

• Make sure your knees are relaxed and are not locked too tight (nor too loose), just comfortably. Now allow your body to move. It will either go forward or backward for the 'yes' or 'no' answer. If your body goes side to side, it means you need to ask a more specific or a better question.

• Please do this three times (3x) for a 'yes' and three times (3x) for a 'no'. Three times is usually enough for your brain to program itself, but you can do it as many times as you need.

• Next, use your name as the question. *"Is my name ________"*.
If you asked your correct name and moved forward, then you are correct. If you asked a wrong name and moved backwards you are also correct (if you answer incorrectly to your name, try saying, "In this life"). *Nic names do not always work because the brain is very, VERY literal.*

• Keep practicing, asking different questions until you know you have 'yes' and 'no' correct. *Sometimes trying with a partner works, where they ask the questions to you.*

• Vitamins are great to use while learning this because the vibratory rate is so high. Ask this question while holding the vitamins to your stomach, "Is this what my body needs to have today?" Try this with 5 – 10 different kinds of vitamins. When you feel confident and you can tell the difference between 'yes' and 'no', try candy.

This muscle testing tool can be used only with a 'yes' or 'no' question. Make sure you are very specific. *After a dream I had, I used Muscle Testing and asked if I should move the school, it said 'no'. Then I asked if I should move all the contents in the school, and it said 'yes'.*

The answers are always **extremely** literal. The building/school (bricks and wood) should not move.

Another time, a question was asked to a bald man if he had hair on his head and his body went forward 'yes'. Literally, he did have hair on his head; facial, ear, brows, eye lashes, etc.

When asking a personal question, your conscious mind knows what answer it wants, so make sure to ask for an "honest and unbiased" answer (Sometimes I add this to the question when I am using Muscle Testing).

You can also do this by thinking of the question and then answering with the muscle testing action. If performing with a friend or family member, touch their shoulder and ask the information about them (surrogate).

You are now ready to ask the correct question to find the order of the personality channels.

When I Muscle Test

1: I ask, if I am on. *"Am I on?"*

• If your body moves backwards, go to the bathroom and/or have a drink of water. Then try again.

• If your body still responds 'no', try again in a day or two. Sometimes if the muscle testing is new information to you and you do not understand it your body will need to adjust to the idea of moving subconsciously.

2: I ask if the personality channels are on one (1) line each. *"Are the personality channels on one line each?"*
• If no, then how many on each line?
  • Test *"2 on a line"*... (what was the answer, yes or no)
  • Test *"3 on a line"*... (what was the answer, yes or no)
  • Test *"4 on a line"*... (what was the answer, yes or no)

3: I ask what order _____ (whoever I am doing) is. Touch the person's shoulder that you are testing for or have them use muscle testing themselves. *"Is _____'s first channel Audio?"* Wait to find the answer.
• If no...
  • *"Is _____'s first channel Knower?"* Wait to find out the answer. If no...
  • *"Is _____'s first channel Visual?"* Wait to find out the answer. If no...
  • *"Is _____'s first channel Feeler?"*
• If yes, then move on to the next channel order until all the channels are tested (Audio, Knower, Visual & Feeler – it will not matter which one you start with).
  • *"Is _____'s second channel Knower?"* Wait to find out the answer.

4: Continue until you have all four channels
• *"Is _____'s third channel Knower?"* Wait to find out the answer. If no...
• *"Is _____'s fourth channel Knower?"*

Most people have a single channel on one line, but they may have two or more on one line with one or more lines blank.

5: As a practitioner I also ask if this was since birth. *"Is this the order _____ was born with?"*
• If not,
  • *"Which order did _____ have at birth?"* Go through the process again.

You can also ask if they had any more and at what age. Personality channels may change with traumatic events; parents splitting up, moving to a new school or city, death of a loved one, physical & emotional trauma, etc.

I can only seem to do Muscle Testing once, since my ego knows that I have tested for the person earlier and I do not want to be wrong if I test a second time. If they test themselves it should always be the same.

Test #3 – Eye Movement

Eye Accessing Chart

This will be as if you are looking at the person (imagine the smiley face below is the person you are looking at).

Their right...Your left **Their left...Your right**

Which direction are their eyes facing?

Meanings of the direction of eye movements

Visuals will look like this, when asked a question

Visual Remembered
• the person is remembering a visual memory
•*Looking up to their left / your right*

Visual Constructed
• the person is creating a visual image. (Not real)
• *Looking up to their right / your left*

Audios will look like this, when asked a question

Auditory Remembered
• the person is remembering hearing a memory
• *Looking across to their left / your right*

Auditory Constructed
• the person is creating a heard sound, (Not real)
•*Looking across to their right / your left*

Feelers will look like this, when asked a question

Kinesthetic
• the person is feeling a memory
•*Looking down to their right / your left*

Knowers will look like this, when asked a question

Self talk

• Can be a sign movement for Knower

• the person is usually repeating in their mind what you just said.

• *Looking down to their left / your right*

Knowing

• the person is remembering a fact

• *Looking straight at you*

Some questions to ask to test their eye movements

A person may do more than one eye movement with any one question (a baby will have to be older to be able to answer you honestly, probably at least the age of four or five).

Ask all the questions, but make sure to watch where their eyes are moving,

Note: check very quickly or use a second person to watch while you read. Subconsciously the first place they look is always their first channel, but once they start to consciously think about the question their eyes will start to change direction.

Some Channel Questions to Ask

Direction they looked

Visual Remembered

What color is_____? _____________________

What does_____look like? _____________________

Can you see_____? _____________________

Visual Constructed

Can you imagine the view from the moon? _____________________

What color would you like your bedroom to be? _____________________

Imagine a creature that's half_____and half _____.? _____________________

Audio remembered

Can you hear_____? _____________________

Can you recall the sound of_____? _____________________

What is something you say to yourself? _____________________

Audio constructed

Combine the sound of_____with _____? _____________________

Can you hear the sound of _____ changing into _____? _____________________

Can you hear _____ and _____ at the same time? _____________________

Feeler

Can you recall the feeling of _____? _____________________

How does _____ feel to you? _____________________

Do you feel the sensation of _____? _____________________

Knower

Any of the previous questions, but they instantly answered and never blinked or looked away. They just looked straight at you (possibly they looked down to the right – self talk).

***Note**: The answer to your question is not really important, what direction their eyes moved is.

TEST #4 – WORD/LISTENING SKILLS EXERCISE

If you listen to the words you or others use you can tell the first channel. The words will give you the answer to which channel a person uses most (the first or main channel). Words like *listen, feel, know,* and *see* are a few of the words people use. These words will describe which personality channel is being used – Audio, Knower, Visual, or Feeler.

Examples:

Visual	Audio	Feeler	Knower
look	listen	smooth	think
clear	say	firm	believe
focus	clicked	cold	understand
see	rings a bell	blown away	suppose
bright	whisper	warm	consider
vague	noise	cool	remember
watch	hear that	how are you	know

Examples of word use while hungry

- A hamburger would sure look good right now. **Visual** Channel
- A hamburger sure sounds good right now. **Audio** Channel
- I know I want a hamburger. **Knower** Channel
- I feel like having a hamburger. **Feeler** Channel

Or while learning

- Can you tell me more details? **Audio** Channel
- Can you draw me a picture? **Visual** Channel
- Let me try. **Feeler** Channel
- I will need to think about that. **Knower** Channel

Or emotional expression

• Saying, I love you. **Audio** Channel
• Buying a gift. **Visual** Channel
• Giving a kiss, hug, or pat on the back (maybe a punch). **Feeler** Channel
• May express affection and then backs off, or would say if asked "You know I love you". **Knower** Channel

Test #5 – Pictures: Look through your photos

Candid photos are best…

Can you tell just by looking at the picture which channel each child is? One is a **knower/visual**, one is an **audio**, and one is a **visual/feeler.** The child on the left has her mouth open to talk (audio), the middle child is looking directly at the camera and is smiling on cue (knower/visual), and the third child on the right is playing with toys (feeler) and looking at the girls (visual). Over twenty years later and this is still how these kids (adults) are now.

People's actions in candid shots will tell you their main channel.

Some examples:

• Talking, playing music, acting = Audio

• Action, fitness, running around, building or touching = Feeler

• Reading, researching on the computer, science projects or hates pictures taken = Knower

• Hair and clothes perfectly matched, room organized tidy, materialistic items = Visual

Test #6 – Written Quiz (For ages 12 and up)

Circle the best answer – a, b, c, or d. You can also ask another person the question to get their answers.

Complete this test to find out what order your Personality Channels of Communication are.
Note: this is only a quiz and is as good or truthful as you marked it.

If a person thinks about the question too long and does not circle the first one(s) that jumps out at them, then they probably circled the wrong answer. You want your subconscious to answer. Yes, you can circle more than one answer per question. No matter what, have some fun...

Circle a, b, c, or d for each question.
If you really do have more than one answer for a question, indicate which one is more important.

1) Do you...
a. See everything in pictures
b. Like to talk
c. Touch everything
d. Like to take your time

2) When you are on the phone, how do you like to communicate?
a. You would rather have the real person in front of you
b. You do all of the talking on the phone
c. You like to doodle
d. You don't call people unless necessary

3) When talking to someone in person, do you...
a. Like to make eye contact
b. Just want to be told the facts
c. Talk with your hands
d. Already know what they are going to say

4) When you are on vacation, what do you like to do?
a. Sight seeing
b. Talk to the locals
c. Go for walks or hikes
d. Find out all about the area first

5) In your free or spare time, do you...
a. Watch TV
b. Chat or text a friend
c. Keep busy
d. Research information or read

6) How do you like being shown love?
a. A bought gift or flowers
b. Cards and being told I love you
c. With touch; hugs & kisses
d. You just know

7) You learn something new by...
a. Being shown
b. Reading about it
c. Being hands on and just doing it
d. Extensively researching

8) Do you like books that...
a. Let you imagine the people and places
b. Are factual, with no spelling mistakes
c. Triggers your emotions
d. Are educational

9) When reading a book do you...
a. Imagine everything in color
b. Notice spelling mistakes
c. Laugh, cry, and get mad just as the character does
d. Have a dictionary to check the meaning of words

10) When using instructions (sewing patterns, appliance manuals, etc.) do you...

a. Need pictures
b. Read the directions to verify and follow one step at a time
c. Just jump in and start without reading or looking at the pictures
d. Read all the information (maybe more than once), and then proceed

11) A reply you say when you agree with someone.

a. I can see that
b. Sounds good
c. That feels right
d. I understand

12) When you have done a good job and are being congratulated, would you like...

a. A gift or plaque
b. Verbal or written acknowledgement
c. A handshake or pat on the back
d. Anything, if given in private

13) When lost and in need of directions, do you...

a. Need a map drawn of what types of buildings are near, including their color
b. Need street names, left/right, North/South, miles/kilometers
c. Just keep walking or driving around until you've found it
d. Research & print the location ahead of time to avoid getting lost in the first place

14) To really believe something you need to...

a. See it
b. Read about it
c. Touch it
d. Study it

15) Success means...
a. Prestigious or beautiful possessions
b. Money in the bank
c. Having money in your pocket and being comfortable
d. Long term security

16) In a conversation with a friend, do you...
a. Wander from topic
b. Need everyone listening
c. Talk with your hands or with animated gestures
d. Engage in familiar topics

17) When putting on clothes for the day, do you...
a. Instantly match clothes and accessories (sock colors have to match)
b. Prefer brand names
c. Put on the first thing you touch
d. Try on a couple of things before deciding

18) Your belongings in your bedroom...
a. Are pretty and have a special location
b. Revolve around the computer and stereo
c. Are very comfortable
d. Are practical

19) When telling someone about your bike or vehicle, do you...
a. Tell them what it looks like
b. Talk about the make and model
c. Talk about how it handles and how fast it goes
d. Talk about practical details and maintenance

20) Sleeping, do you dream in...
a. Color
b. Hear different sounds
c. Fly, run, or ride (or try to)
d. Do not usually remember dreaming

Totals
Now add up how many A, B, C, or D's you have circled.

A ______ A = Visual
B ______ B = Audio
C ______ C = Feeler
D ______ D = Knower

So, what is the order of your Personality Channels?
Your highest number goes in the 1st row and so forth.

A ______
B ______
C ______
D ______

If you have any that are equal, they go on the same row. It is okay to have blank rows.

Examples:
If all were different numbers, then it would look something like this:
A __8__
B __3__
C __6__
D __4__

Yours: (write your name here)
1st channel / language: __Visual__ ______ ______ ______
2nd channel / language: __Feeler__ ______ ______
3rd channel / language: __Knower__ ______
4th channel / language: __Audio__

Or if visual and feeler were the same number, then it would look like this:

A ___7___
B ___3___
C ___7___
D ___4___

Yours: (write your name here)______
1st channel / language: _Visual_ _Feeler_ ______ ______
2nd channel / language: _Knower_ ______ ______
3rd channel / language: _Audio_ ______
4th channel / language: ______

Or if visual and feeler were the same number but less than knower, then it would look like this:

A ___5___
B ___3___
C ___5___
D ___8___

Yours: (write your name here)
1st channel / language: _Knower_ ______ ______ ______
2nd channel / language: _Visual_ _Feeler_ ______
3rd channel / language: _Audio_ ______
4th channel / language: ______

Or if visual, feeler, knower, and audio were all the same number, and then it would look something like this (three extra letters were circled):

A ___6___
B ___6___
C ___6___
D ___6___

Yours: (write your name here)
1st channel / language: Visual Knower Feeler Audio
2nd channel / language: _______ _______ _______
3rd channel / language: _______ _______
4th channel / language: _______

Now it is your turn

Yours: ____________________
1st channel / language: _______ _______ _______ _______
2nd channel / language: _______ _______ _______
3rd channel / language: _______ _______
4th channel / language: _______

Partner: ____________________
1st channel / language: _______ _______ _______ _______
2nd channel / language: _______ _______ _______
3rd channel / language: _______ _______
4th channel / language: _______

Child: ____________________
1st channel / language: _______ _______ _______ _______
2nd channel / language: _______ _______ _______
3rd channel / language: _______ _______
4th channel / language: _______

Child: ____________________
1st channel / language: _______ _______ _______ _______
2nd channel / language: _______ _______ _______
3rd channel / language: _______ _______
4th channel / language: _______

Child: ____________________
1st channel / language: _______ _______ _______ _______
2nd channel / language: _______ _______ _______
3rd channel / language: _______ _______
4th channel / language: _______

Mom: ____________________
1st channel / language: _______ _______ _______ _______
2nd channel / language: _______ _______ _______
3rd channel / language: _______ _______
4th channel / language: _______

Dad: ____________________
1st channel / language: _______ _______ _______ _______
2nd channel / language: _______ _______ _______
3rd channel / language: _______ _______
4th channel / language: _______

Friend: ____________________
1st channel / language: _______ _______ _______ _______
2nd channel / language: _______ _______ _______
3rd channel / language: _______ _______
4th channel / language: _______

Other: ____________________
1st channel / language: _______ _______ _______ _______
2nd channel / language: _______ _______ _______
3rd channel / language: _______ _______
4th channel / language: _______

Other: ____________________
1st channel / language: _______ _______ _______ _______
2nd channel / language: _______ _______ _______
3rd channel / language: _______ _______
4th channel / language: _______

Other: ____________________
1st channel / language: _______ _______ _______ _______
2nd channel / language: _______ _______ _______
3rd channel / language: _______ _______
4th channel / language: _______

How to Understand your Personality Channels of Communication

Now that you know your order,
you might want to understand what the order means...

If you took the #6 Written Quiz, here are examples to understand the order of Your Personality Channels of Communication.

If the order of your Personality Channels of Communication or someone you know is:

Example #1
1st Channel:Visual
2nd Channel: Feeler
3rd Channel: Knower
4th Channel: Audio

***Note:** *Channels under the line mean that you do not usually use these. You can refer to under the line as opposite information or things you do not do.*
Example: *Audio now means to hate talking on the phone.*

The first channel is a person's main channel, and the two channels above the line will determine how a person loves and learns. The person in example #1 would be very materialistic, spontaneous (one who would jump right into something if it looked and felt good), would love to be busy making things or doing things, hates to waste time thinking about something, and would not like talking on the phone.

Example #2 - All channels on one line
1st Channel: Visual, Feeler, Knower, Audio
2nd Channel: *Blank*
3rd Channel: *Blank*
4th Channel: *Blank*

These people would be a similar to Example #1, although they may now exhibit all the channel's traits equally. But because knower and audio are now above the line, the person will like to talk on the phone and spend time thinking about something. And they will not be quite as spontaneous and materialistic as Example #1 because the audio and knower traits will tame the urge.

What is the worst part of having all your channels open at once?

People with all four channels equally have it the hardest... Imagine four radio stations playing at the same time. Hard to hear any one station individually, and all you would get is noise. It can be too much stimuli at once and because the brain cannot usually control which one to listen to it will start to try to block the noise out or shut the noise out completely. A person with all four channels open equally may seem to be withdrawn, have ADD Attention Deficit Disorder, or be autistic.

To overcome this, a person needs to know their first channel and then concentrate on that particular channel for learning and love. They can do all of them, but they need to learn to concentrate on the main one.

Knowing your family, friends, student or business associate's order of the Personality Channels will help you understand and communication with them better. When I found out my family's order of the Personality Channels (especially their main one), I changed the way I spoke to and treated them. Also, it's important to know that your friends and family are not trying to irritate you. They were born with their channels, or an experience created them, and they really only know their own way to communicate...not yours!

I created my channels to all be on top of each other, I also know how to turn them off and on at will.

Had to put this in...Here is one that I love, instead of ADD
(ADOS – Attention Deficit... Oh Shiny; a good laugh for the Visuals)

Combinations and/or Reactions to each other

Example #1 - Best Combination

Can be in any channel combination

When the 1st & 2nd Channels are opposite it is the BEST combination ever!
(Even more so when FV or VF are together, and KA or AK are together)

Yours	Theirs
V	A
A	V
K	K
F	F

Benefits:

- Both of you like to talk
- Both like pretty things and have order in the house
- Both love and understand the same
- Both do not need much time to make a decision
- Both may not complete all tasks

Problems or Issues:

- Not much of anything
- Sometimes too loud of a household. ie: talking, music, TV

Example #2 - Worst Combination

Can be in any channel combination

When there are no matching channels, this is the WORST combination!

Yours	Theirs
F	K
V	A
A	V
K	F

Benefits:

- Nothing! There is no common channel of communication.

Problems or Issues:

- Do not love the same
- Do not learn the same
- In this case you are spontaneous and the

other person needs lots of time
- You are a doer and other person seems lazy
- You like everything in its place and other person is messy

So many issues here! This is where it takes a very special person to really do their research and want to fix the problems.

Example #3

Yours		Theirs
F	——	F
A	——	A
K		K
V		V

Benefits:
- Really easy to understand each other but may butt heads
- Seem to get along, but over time may start to compete with one another
- Both learn exactly the same way and love the same way

Problems or Issues:
- Competitive
- May need to respect the age difference, if there is one

Example #4

Yours		Theirs
A		K
K	／	V
V		F
F		A

Benefits:
- Both can get along because of their connection to K (knower).
- Both are late a lot and need time to think about something (them more than you).
- Both do not like exercise or doing much with their hands
- The person who is an AK (audio/knower) is a bit of a know it all and probably very loud. They have rules and expect them to be followed.
- The KV (knower/visual) person hates talking and wants to see how to do

something. They will be particular with how they dress. The other person may be intuitive to you.

Problems or Issues:

- You will expect the other person to do everything you say, when you say it
- They will need more time
- You talk and probably yell, and they hate it (Audio is last of their channels)
- They like pretty or flashy things – You don't care about that kind of stuff

Example #5

Yours		Theirs
V		A
F	———	F
K		K
A		V

Benefits:

- The two can get along because of their connection to F (feeler).
- Both like hugs and doing something
- Both do not take their time

Problems or Issues:

- You are more spontaneous then they are
- They talk a lot
- They do not care how they dress
- They are messy – You like to see everything in its correct place
- They need to talk or listen to music all the time and you don't like it
- You don't like spending money on designer brands or the 'IN THINGS'– They do!

Families

Example #1

Parent #1	Parent #2	Child #1	Child #2	Child #3
F	K	A	V	A
A	A	K	F	F
V	V	F	K	K
K	F	V	A	V

• Parents get along but have their differences, mostly in when something is done.
• Child #1 and Parent #2 get along the best
• Child #3 and Parent #1 get along best (it will seem like the parents have their favorites)
• Child #2 can get along with Parent #1 but not with Parent #2
• Child #2 gets along with Child #3 but not with Child #1
• Child #1 and #3 can get along
• Child #2 will be the issue; he or she will learn and love differently than the other kids, and will want different toys than the other two

Example #2 - Changing only Parent #1

Parent #1	Parent #2	Child #1	Child #2	Child #3
F	K	A	V	A
V	A	K	F	F
K	V	F	K	K
A	F	V	A	V

• Parents are probably divorced or fight a lot
• Parent # 1 gets along great with child #2, can get along with child #3, but not with child #1
• Parent #2 gets along great with child #1 and pretty good with child #3, but not child #2
• Child #3 gets along with both other children
• Child #1 and #2 do not get along

Example #3 - Changing Parent #2 and Child #3

Parent #1	Parent #2	Child #1	Child #2	Child #3
F	V	A	V	F
V	F	K	F	V
K	K	F	K	K
A	A	V	A	A

- Parents get along great
- Parent #1 gets along best with child #2 and very well with #3, but not at all with child #1
- Parent #2 gets along best with child #3, very well with #2, but not at all with child #1
- Child #2 and #3 get along great together
- Child #1 is the so called 'black sheep' and probably fights with or ignores everyone. He/she would leave home as early as possible and may never talk to the rest of the family again

Note: Any combination where one person is different than the rest of the family there is going to be turmoil. All of you would really need to learn to communicate with the odd channeled person if a healthy relationship is going to continue.

Constance's Family

Following are my family's channels, and how knowing these made a huge difference in my relationship with my children and husband. *I muscle tested this information in 1999 when my daughter was in grade four and my son was in grade five.*

Note: Remember, the first and second channel will tell you how a person acts, learns, and how they love.

Constance's Family's Order of the Personality Channels in 1999

Channel	Constance	Husband	Son	Daughter
1st	Visual	Feeler	Visual	Audio
2nd	Feeler	Visual	Feeler	Knower/Feeler
3rd	Knower	Audio	Knower	Visual
4th	Audio	Knower	Audio	

As you can see, my daughter would have been the outcast, or as some would say 'black sheep'. It's very noticeable that she is different than the rest of us. My Son had the same order of channels as me, and my husband was very similar. I will explain each of my family's channels by starting with myself.

1999 Constance

1st Channel - Visual

• I am a very materialistic (and still am); I need to see everything to believe it.
• I have a place for all my belongings and, God forbid, if you do not put it back in its correct place...
• I learn by watching (visual) and doing (feeler) at the same time.
• If I am sewing I just follow the pictures, and if I really can't get it I will read the directions and pray I understand what they mean.

• Cooking works the same way. I love the pictures in cookbooks, therefor I can make it look the same way, or at least know what the outcome should look like.
• I usually buy books based on what the front cover looks like.
• My clothes have to match!!!!
• I am a bit of a tidy freak (I notice anything out of place).
• I do things very spontaneously. If it looks good and feels good, I do it without thinking (notice my knower is under the line).
• I need to be given gifts or something I can see to be shown I am loved. • When my husband does dishes for me, builds me furniture, or fixes something for me, I know he loves me.
• When I talk, I often talk about three or more things at once (because I am afraid I will forget what I wanted to say). I can see everything in my head that needs to be said.
• I love stories and can see the pictures in my head like a movie.
• I dream in color.
• I can watch a black and white TV, and in my mind I have turned it into color (I remember once someone on TV saying "what a beautiful green dress", and I had imagined a purple one. It kind of wrecked my image; green was not my favorite color).
• I love to draw and paint, or create any kind of art (visual and feeler).
• I love to see new places.
• I need to see and touch my money (chairs, vehicles, etc.)
• I used to do industrial sewing as a living and could see my accomplishments.
• Words might look wrong even if they are written correctly.
• I use sticky notes to remind me of an important message or I would call myself and leave a phone message (out of sight out of mind).

2nd Channel - Feeler

(Some of my feeler points were said above in my visual)

• I love to be doing things, I have a hard time sitting still (feeler) and sometimes I do two or more things at once). Example: watching TV (visual) and knitting (feeler).
• I can have people come very close to me and do not usually mind being touched.
• I can feel other people's moods.
• I do not mind getting my hands dirty; I will jump right in.
• I love the taste of food.
• I do not like the feeling or effects of alcohol or drugs.

Under the Line

You have just read detailed information on my Visual and Feeler traits (they are above the line), and you will have noticed the Knower and Audio traits are under the line. These are two traits that I do not do naturally. Meaning they are under the line and they do not come easily to me.

3rd Channel - Knower

• I get frustrated with people who cannot make up their minds quickly. I do not need much time to make a decision; it takes me seconds (no joke).
• If I am not shown how to do something, it seems like it takes longer for me to understand something new.
• I am self conscious of telling people anything, just in case I am not correct.
• I hate being alone.

4th Channel - Audio

• I hate to talk on the phone or write letters. *In grade nine I froze when I was public speaking in front of my class (so embarrassing), and my main reason for quitting college when I was eighteen was because after a few public speaking classes my original group of eight peers combined with another class and turned into thirty. I could not handle that many people looking at me when I spoke.*
• I hate a loud voice or yelling.
• I never read the fine print.

• I take weeks and weeks to read a book.

My Husband as of 1999

1st Channel - Feeler

• (Of course I would marry a woodworker; he could always show me love)
• He is always busy.
• Loves to play sports and exercise; baseball, tennis, skiing, going for walks, doing sit ups, etc.
• Needs to be touched to feel loved (not just sex).
• If I need his total attention, I have to touch his arm.
• He has to feel that something is a good idea (gut instinct).
• Learns by just doing it (feeler) and also by watching (visual) at the same time.
• Learns by trial and error.
• The books he reads need to make him feel like he is on an adventure.
• Puts on whatever is comfortable (but does care what it looks like).
• Does not leave anything in the same place.
• Will drop his clothes on the floor (especially at night, when no one will see).
• Can be spontaneous as long as it feels good.
• He likes to feel secure and that he always has access to his money.
• Has to feel useful and needed.

2nd Channel - Visual

• Materialistic (as long as it feels good). Needs to see to believe it.
• Loves stories and can see the pictures in his head.
• Dreams in color.
• Can draw and paint.

Under the line

3rd Channel - Audio

• Hardly talks on the phone, never writes letters.
• In person can start to ramble and cannot always tell when he has gone on too long.
• Hardly reads the fine print.
• Takes a very long time to read a book.

• Messy handwriting

4th Channel - Knower

• Takes forever to understand something, unless he does it.

• Hates being alone.

My Son as of 1999

1st Channel - Visual

• Materialistic; needs to see everything to believe it.

• Has a place for all belongings and God forbid if you move it or touch it.

• Learns by watching (visual) and by doing it (feeler) at the same time. *When he was about two and a half, my Mom bought a Little Tikes slide. He saw the picture on the box and started to put it together by himself.*

• Show him how to do something and he can copy it.

• Very picky about the clothes he wears, and at a very young age he would not wear what I wanted him to.

• Very tidy.

• Spontaneous.

• Loves gifts or something he can see to be shown he is loved. Had one favorite toy for years.

• Loves to watch TV.

• Talks fast.

• Loves stories.

• Dreams in color.

• Loves to draw and paint, or make any kind of art (visual and feeler).

• Loves to see new places.

2nd Channel - Feeler

• Loves to play video games.

• He loves to be doing things. *(ADD. In grade three, his teacher said he had attention Deficit Disorder and wanted him on Ritalin. I never put him on it, I just kept him busy)*

• Always busy. He has about a fifteen minute attention span.

• Is a lover, not a fighter.

• Loves to try anything.

• Loves food.
• Touched things he did not understand. *(Even when he shouldn't have)*
• He was learning two languages at a time to keep him busy at school, English and French

Under the line

3rd Channel - Knower

• Gets frustrated with people who cannot make up their minds quickly.
• If not shown how to do something, it will take longer for him to understand.
• Self conscious of telling people anything, just in case he is not correct. Hates being alone.

4th Channel - Audio

• Hates to talk on the phone or write letters.
• Hates a loud voice or yelling.
• Takes time to read a book (If you could get him to read at that age).

My Daughter as of 1999

1st Channel - Audio

• Loves to talk (24/7).
• Loves to call her friends on the phone, ever since kindergarten.
• Loves to be chatting on the computer (Texting wasn't a thing yet).
• Will yell to be heard.
• Finds reading boring, they're just words *(When she was in grade three, I found out why she hated to read. She did not see pictures when she read and could not imagine what was in the story. I found this out when I was driving the kids to school and her brother was telling me about what the castle looked like in one of the Harry Potter books he was reading. All of a sudden she yelled at him to stop lying, there were no pictures of a castle in the book. This took me by surprise. I then bought one of Mary Kate and Ashley's books from their hit TV show 'Two of a Kind" (It was one of her favorite shows). Since she had seen the TV show before, it was easy for her to read the book and enjoy it because the memory/ pictures were still in her mind.*

• She loved being told "I love you" in words or in writing. I use to write her notes and put them into her lunch bag.
• She was learning two languages, English and French, and is very good at both.
• She now reads any new information and can learn it easily from written format.

2nd Channel - Knower

• Gets frustrated with people easily.
• Once she knows something she knows it, and will tell you all about it.
• Needs a bit of time to understand something if she did not read it.
• Has no problem being alone (This is only a problem if the Knower trait is under the line).
• Thinks things out.

2nd Channel - Feeler

(I think she developed this just to survive in our family)

• Loves her animals.
• Likes to be busy.
• Loves to try anything.
• Used to come and sit on our laps for a hug.

Under the line

3rd Channel - Visual

• Never cares about what she wears;would even wear two different colored socks.
• Doesn't care where she leaves things.
• Hardly ever watches TV.
• Does not need stories and is quick to the point.
• Struggles with make-up. (It took years, but she finally got better at it.).

To summarize my family

The most important channel is the first one, which is also the easiest to figure out.

1st Channel

Constance	Husband	Son	Daughter
Visual	Feeler	Visual	Audio

You can figure out these channels even by listening to the words a person uses.

Constance	Husband	Son	Daughter
See you later	Let's go for a walk	Let's watch TV	Talk to you soon

You can also discover them through their learning style

Constance	Husband	Son	Daughter
Seeing	Doing	Seeing	Listening/Reading

How to make sense of the information gathered

Channel	Constance	Husband	Son	Daughter
1st	Visual	Feeler	Visual	Audio
2nd	Feeler	Visual	Feeler	Knower/Feeler
3rd	Knower	Audio	Knower	Visual
4th	Audio	Knower	Audio	

My Husband and I, as a couple, get along extremely well. We can communicate well and understand each other's channels. He, being a Feeler/Visual, and I being a Visual/Feeler are not exactly the same, so we do not compete with each other, but have enough in common that we can understand one another.

I had to learn to touch him more, so he could experience love his way. I would hold his hand or arm when we walked, I would rub his back, touch him when I talked to him, or we would sit on our love seat instead of the couch when watching TV so I could touch his feet with mine.

Interesting story, we moved into a new house and the way we had to set up the TV and furniture was different then the last few years. At first, my husband and I sat on different couches, and then after a few days he came over to the love seat I was on and chose to sit there instead of the other seat he started with, just to be closer to me.

• My husband had to learn to show me love by doing dishes without me asking, building me things, fixing things, giving flowers, or giving gifts.
• My son and husband get along very well, since my son's channels are just like mine. I have to be a bit more careful with my son because we are so much alike. We compete with each other too much, thinking only one of us is correct and it is never the other person. We sometimes make the mistake of believing we know what each other is thinking.
• My son always needs a fifteen minute notice before leaving or going somewhere. **Example**: *"We are leaving in fifteen minutes"*, then another reminder five minutes before we were leaving. I would say, *"Five minutes"*. Then, when we were leaving I would say, *"Okay, we are leaving now"*. It worked every time without any issues.

• If I wanted him to do chores or errands, I would give him a time limit to have them done by. **Example**: (the day before) *"By 8:00 pm tomorrow your room needs to be cleaned"*. The next morning, I would remind him *"By 8:00 pm your room needs to be cleaned"*. If I needed it quickly I would say, *"I need it finished in the next two hours"*.
• In regards to my daughter (who is the one that I thank God that I learned all this personality channels information, especially when she was younger), she was so different than the rest of the family. The three of us love movies and food while she does not; she loves music and her friends. She does not understand our jokes and does not like to play games with us.

• When I realized how she needed to receive love, I changed many things that I did or expected from her. I used to freak out and ground her for calling her friends and talking to them for so long. After understanding more about the personality channels, I went and bought another phone and put it in her bedroom. I also added call waiting to our phone plan and told her she could talk all she wanted so long as she answered the call waiting and was off the phone by 8:00 pm (back then it was etiquette for her age). As soon as I had the money, I bought her a computer with internet so she could chat online (I loved it. The phone stopped ringing and I did not have to hear her talking anymore).

• I began to watch what words I used, because not only did she listen, but she was also very sensitive to every spoken word. Sometimes she would start to cry at the slightest thing I'd said. Often, I wouldn't even know what I'd said, and when she'd tell me I was surprised that what I'd said and what she'd heard were two very different interpretations. I had to learn to become much more literal when using my words!!! Notice the language I used to describe how I reacted – I used the word *watch*. I am a true visual).

• As a family we started to take turns choosing activities so that everyone had a chance to do what they enjoyed, even if it was not what the rest of the family wanted to do. I started asking the kids what they wanted for their birthday and Christmas so that I wasn't guessing, projecting, or assuming (especially since what I liked was definitely not what my daughter liked).

• I learned to turn around and watch her talk so I could focus on listening and not tune her out (I am still working on that one). I let her listen to loud music until my bedtime since she did not sleep as much as the rest of us. I bought her a cell phone in grade seven so I could get a hold of her, especially because she liked being out rather than being at home with us.

In the end, both of my children say they love how we let them grow up, and their friends have commented many times on how different we are, wishing they grew up in our family or had parents as understanding.

How to Communicate with a Different Personality Channel than You…

You were born with your channel order, or maybe because of your environment (a special situation – usually emotional trauma) you had to change your order. In any case, it is as much a part of you as your arm or foot. Just as you have your own personal order of channels, so do others around you.

If you are an adult and the other person is a child, then it is your responsibility to adjust or at least try to accept the other person's personality traits. Remember, they are just different than your own, so try to get along as best you can. But, with an adult to adult you have a few choices:

- Walk away
- Educate yourself
- Educate them
- Tolerate the time together and then move on
- Try, for a moment, to be like them (try this!!!)
- **See** what they see while they are talking to you
    - Take a breath and touch between your eyebrows when listening to them
- **Hear** what they hear while they are talking to you
    - Take a breath and touch behind your ear when listening to them
- **Feel** like they feel while they are talking to you
    - Take a breath and touch your stomach when listening to them
- **Know** what they know while they are talking to you
    - Take a breath and touch the top of your head when listening to them

This may seem silly or strange, but you may be amazed at what a difference it will make in communicating!

If it really matters and you truly want or need to adjust your channels, because of a child or partner, then it may be worth the effort. It takes a lot of practice and hard work to change a personality channel order and the traits that come with them. **It can be done!**

How to Develop or Change Your Order of Personality Channels

An Actor or Actress can change their persona with every new role they play!

In every new role an actor plays, the new character he or she portrays usually has a very different personality. A great example is Johnny Depp. It has been said that, *"Johnny Depp is perhaps one of the most versatile actors of his day and age in Hollywood"*. Wow, can that man change his character! So much so that there are many times it takes me a few moments to figure out that it's him playing the role. He has a knack for changing his whole personality to fit the character he is playing.

Meaning, it can be done and usually not as often as Johnny Depp needs to.

What can make a change?

I have found over the years that a major move, a divorce, losing a loved one, or anything emotionally traumatic can change the order of the channels.

On purpose, I was trying to make my channels to change so that all channels were equal to each other.

	Birth	**2002**	**2006**
Channel	**Constance**	**Constance**	**Constance**
1st	Visual	Visual	Visual, Feeler, Knower, Audio
2nd	Feeler	Feeler/Knower	
3rd	Knower	Audio	
4th	Audio		

2008
Constance
All languages on top of each other

How did I do it?

To understand all of my students I had to bring my Knower and Audio up over the line. Once over the line, my brain took notice of the channel's qualities and paid attention to outside stimulus. I personally wanted to understand all of my students. I wanted to be a better teacher and be able to teach to that channel or learning style. It was very important to me.

To change a channel on purpose you need to practice that quality (see the individual traits page for more ideas).

Visual: art; draw, paint, design etc.
Feeler: hands on; build something (maybe out of wood or lego), cooking
Audio: reading, typing, talking
Knower: to take more time to decide something, analyze the situation

Practice, practice, and more practice. This can take years to change.

To Change Your Personality Channels or develop the other Channels

Whether you want to change them completely or be more acute, you have to practise them in everyday trivial things such as reading, writing, speaking, thinking, problem solving, touching, doing, perceiving, and drawing. Whatever channel you want to enhance, you must incorporate it into your everyday life.

When I started teaching, I paid attention to my students and the differences in how they learned.

For some students I had to change the way I explained things

- While I described the procedures, some students could just listen to me and learn
- Other students needed me to demonstrate
- Some had to actually do it or have it done on them
- And others just needed time to understand it all

Understanding someone's channel is extremely important. You will find it so much easier to get along with people if you enjoy a rapport and understand where they are coming from.

I have had many students and clients whose channels have changed, but not because they meant to. Using the Muscle Testing Technique, I could find out if they have had more than one order of channels over the years.

I tested their birth language (the order of channels they had at birth), and then I tested at what age they changed to a new order. I have found that this type of change was usually due to something very emotional happening in their life, be it a move where they left their friends, a divorce in the family, or because of any other traumatic experience. Their brain seemed to have changed and adapted to their new circumstances or surroundings and the person changed how they communicated.

Example #1

Channel	Original birth channel	New order
1st	Feeler	Audio
2nd	Audio	Feeler
3rd	Visual	Visual
4th	Knower	Knower

• This person needed to talk more and become pickier in details

Example #2

Channel	Original birth channel	New order
1st	Feeler	Audio
2nd	Audio	Visual
3rd	Visual	Feeler
4th	Knower	Knower

• This person needed to not feel and to become pickier in details. They probably told people bluntly how it is and does not care about other people's feelings.

Example #3

Channel	Original birth channel	New order
1st	Knower	Feeler
2nd	Feeler	Audio
3rd	Audio	Visual
4th	Visual	Knower

• This person became less cautious and more spontaneous, busier, detail oriented, now likes to talk, and will hug and tell you they love you. They will also spend their money faster than before.

I have witnessed a person who had changed their channels five times in their life.

As said before, I have personally worked very hard to intentionally change my channels. This has taken me years to achieve. I needed to understand my student's and client's channels. Not to mention I am also teaching this information, so how good would I really be if my Audio and Knower was not sufficient?

Constance today

Imagine all four languages on top of each other. Visual, Feeler, Audio, and Knower all on the first row overlapping. Also you may have noticed my Audio and Knower switched places of importance.

To achieve this I have been writing, taking classes, slowing down and reading the fine print, chatting more on the internet (my friends would say 'yeah right'), taking more time to make a decision, using different lingo, like *'I know that'*, *'that sounds good'*, etc.

Over the years, I have been able to help many, many people who were having difficulties understanding themselves or their loved ones. Teaching them how not to judge the other person, but to learn how to use the channels, communicate, and to adjust when need be, bettered their skills for the purpose of work, love, and learning.

Once you have an understanding of the channels and are learning to realize your differences, you might have to change for the time being.

(mostly due to the fact that other people may not have learned this information and don't yet understand the personality channels; therefore, they cannot change to your way).

Many teachers have also noticed that it is much easier to teach a class once they have figured out how their students best learn. All they need to do is demonstrate or explain in all four channels and all of the students should understand.

Just remember: Other people are not acting the way they do just to upset you, it is just how they are and they cannot help it. To change would take years unless something traumatic happened, and then there is no guarantee it would change to your advantage.

Your Persona…
The Mask You Wear

…as the play ended, Cleopatra took a bow. Shivers of delight ran up and down her body as the audience stood, gracing her with an applause of adoration and gratitude as they yearned for an encore… they just wanted more.

Other Books, Workshops, and Seminars in the Series

Your Persona... in Love

Learn to alter your own persona to another person's way, or request love the way you need it given. This is a gift of knowledge that many readers and audiences have found profound.

Your Persona... for the Parent

Learning your child's natural born persona/personality channels will make your life so much easier. For discipline, education, love, and understanding what they need, so you can help them become the best they can be.

Your Persona... in Education

hen a teacher and/or parent understands the student's main personality channel and caters to it, the child excels in their studies!

Your Persona... the Afterlife

or those of you who are fascinated with mediumship, knowing a person's main channel in life will tell you how to contact them.

Your Persona... for the Psychic

Are you intuitive? Understanding your four personality channels will increase your accuracy!

Your Persona... in Wealth

How do you make, spend, and save money? Understanding your four personality channels will help your pocketbook!

Your Persona... in your Occupation

Do you want to be better at work and take steps towards the job of your dreams? Then you will need to know how to adjust your personality channels to remain flexible in the industry, being the best you can be!

Your Persona... for the Teenager

Learn all about yourself so you can love, laugh, and enjoy the journey!

Your Persona... for the Therapist

It may mean the difference between a great day and a crazy day. Learning the four personality channels will increase your rapport with your clients -a slight adjustment your Persona might be all you need!

Your Persona... in Health

Your main personality channel will tell you so many things about your health and how to deal with it.

Visit **www.constancesantego.ca** for workshops, seminars, and books.

Appendices

Bibliography

- Astrology – fire, earth, air, and water
  http://www.trans4mind.com/personal_development/astrology/LearningAstrology/triplicities.htm
- Astrological sign
  http://zodiac-signs-astrology.com/
- Ayurvedic Body Types
  http://www.whatsyourdosha.com/
- Body Language - Pease, Allan, and Barbara - 2004
  The Definitive Book of Body Language. New York, New York: Bantam Books
- Colour Spectrums
  First Consultants Inc. Rob Chubb Workshop
- Constance Santego
  (Former Connie Brummet owner of the Canadian Institute of Natural health and Healing)
- Definitions
  Wikipedia
- Four colors: yellow, blue, red, and green
  http://www.personality-and-aptitude-career-tests.com/color-personality-tests.html
  Bolles, Richard N. - 2007 - What Color Is Your Parachute?: Ten Speed Press
- Jungian Types the Four Temperaments
  http://changingminds.org/explanations/preferences/mbti.htm
- Neuro Linguistic Programming NLP
  http://www.bennettstellar.org/
- Muscle Testing
  http://www.kinesiologycollegeofcanada.com/holistictapestri.html
- Myers-Briggs Type Indicator
- Photos purchased from Istockphoto.com

- Right brained left brained

  http://www.web-us.com/brain/right_left_brain_characteristics.htm
- Somatotypes

  William Sheldon

  http://www.kheper.net/topics/typology/somatotypes.html
- The Four Humors

  http://www.kheper.net/topics/typology/four_humours.html
- Type A / B Personalities

  Created by Meyer Friedman, an American cardiologist
  http://changingminds.org/explanations/preferences/typea_typeb.htm
- Love

  http://www.thefreedictionary.com/love

I truly love to teach and share my knowledge with others.
It makes me so happy when someone comes up to me and shares his or her experience of how my books or workshops have changed their life path for the better.

Shift happens… Create magic,
Constance

Also Available

Constance Santego offers a wide range of Products, Personal Sessions, Retreats, and Educational Workshops.

Soft cover and e-book

The Intuitive Life

A Guide to Self Knowledge & Healing through Psychic Development

Fairy Tales, Dreams and Reality...

Where are you on your path?

Upcoming books

Your Persona...

In Love

Your Persona...

In Education

Your Persona...

In the Afterlife

Angelic Lifestyle

Health & Vibration

Secrets of a Healer Series

For more information on videos or workshops please visit
www.constancesantego.ca

About the Author

Constance Santego is a Canadian businesswoman, author, and artist. She became world renowned for her Inspiration and Manifestation seminars, and self-help books: Intuitive Life, Fairy Tales Dreams & Reality, and Your Persona. Her passion is teaching self-empowerment through self-improvement; emotionally, spiritually, mentally, and physically.

Constance Santego inspires with many of her step-by-step workshops, books, and seminars, taking you on a journey to transform your life and accelerate your path to achieving your dreams.

Shift happens… Create magic!
Constance